an infatuation

fishing

by Tom O'Reilly

Contents

The Infatuation

I am infatuated with angling. Not just one small part, like fishing solely for carp, but with every aspect, from fishing for trout on fresh spring days to stalking pike on frozen winter mornings, even sea fishing for mackerel when the summer sun brings the fish closer to the shore.

In love? Most definitely! Truly addicted, besotted and engrossed. How many times have I asked myself why? The question can only be answered by the gentle bobbing of a float which indicates a hidden world, or by the dry fly slowly drifting downstream…and then, the take. That moment, that split second, that flurry keeps me hooked!

Notes

Notes

But is it just this? Of course not. It's everything that goes with it. The waterscape, the animal life, the natural world, the fishing tackle itself. The small, brightly coloured floats; varnishing the favourite old rod in eager anticipation of when it will flex and strain under a mighty fish; the familiar sound of the ratchet on my best reel; the smell of my old wax jacket; the squeak of rubber waders and the sound of rain on the brolly as it gently taps. Then there is the beautiful high-pitched 'peep' of the kingfisher and the lordly look of the heron; the night fishing camping trips and waking up to a fried breakfast which will be shared with the water rats and a friendly robin. There is the smell of the cold, vibrant stream, rushing and falling over the boulders, the fragrance of fish slime, which is bitter and sweet and can be associated only with a good catch. These are just a fraction of the things which keep me going back year after year to my fishing.

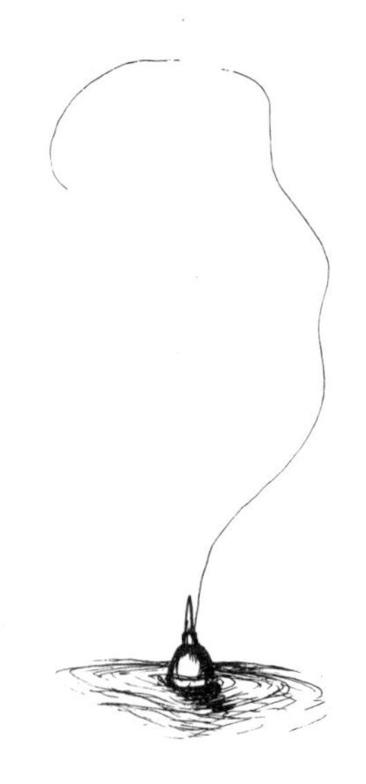

Angling is a sport of a thousand different facets.

Tag Barnes

Notes

Notes

How and where do I begin to try to put into words and pictures my lust for angling? Do I start from my earliest memory or my biggest fish?

No! I'll start at the beginning of the year – spring! When the world seems to be awakening after several months of hibernation, the trees are sprouting new growth and the rivers call.

Spring

Barbel The beginning of spring until the end of the coarse fishing season is a wonderful time for barbel. As the water temperature rises they seem to feed just that little bit more – most coarse fish do the same. Pond fish like the carp slowly warm up after semi-hibernation. If the sun is shining, the river sparkles with energy and new life.

Notes

In the deeper water pools barbel drift silently along the bottom, silhouetted against the sand or gravel. My bait is usually sweetcorn. A ground bait of hemp seed is scattered around. It is presented to the barbel by means of a lead bullet which is slowly moved around the bed of the river as if the hooked bait had been thrown in and didn't have a hook in it. Sometimes, instead of a lead weight I might use a swim feeder stuffed full with maggots to act as ground bait. Lob worms also make an excellent bait.

Aylmers Tryons had a record barbel in 1934 which he caught on a lob worm from the Hampshire Avon. The date was 13 September - the same date on which Richard Walker caught his record carp in 1952. I wonder how many more record-size fish have been caught on this date?

Notes

The barbel is one of the most beautiful of all fish. Its long, streamlined, elegant shape makes its cousin, the carp, look clumsy and squat. I like to use a centre-pin reel while fishing for barbel. It seems somehow very natural – very basic. The line slowly trickles off the drum as the bait rambles downstream. This is where the centre-pin is better than a fixed-spool reel. Casting is quite hard to master, a lot of patience is needed as tangles appear as if by magic, but when a fish is hooked, every movement is felt, unlike a fixed-spool, which absorbs the motion with gears. There is also the fact that you have a certain amount of extra control over the way the line is gathered or taken by a fighting fish. I usually use an eleven-foot, three-piece rod or the old ten-foot Avon design. Although I find the latter to be too short, it is good for close-in work.

Notes

I like to travel light when I'm barbel fishing. It's good to roam about from swim to swim, spending a while at each pitch and finding the fish by looking out for them from high up trees, getting a good vantage point. I don't think I could fish without wearing polarising sunglasses. They are so useful, especially when spotting fish, and of course you should never go fishing without a landing net.

It's strange to think that, just a generation or two ago, the gaffing of coarse fish was very much the done thing. It sends chills down my back to think about how many huge fish died unnecessarily. The same also goes for fish taxidermy. How many of all stuffed specimen fish would have kept on growing to be massive? Would Bob Richards' record Redmire carp have grown to be a fifty-pounder? Or Aylmer Tryon's 14lb 8oz barbel grown to be a twenty-pounder? We'll never know.

Notes

Notes

I like taxidermy as decoration, though. As I write I'm being spied upon by a beautiful kingfisher which I found dead at my local pond and had mounted. A plaster cast of a four-pound tench also watches me – again I found it dead. It's good to preserve such wonderful creatures, but to kill a specimen-size fish, or indeed any other animal, just to be cased is very sad. Luckily the camera, to a great extent, has replaced the practice of mounting. A quick shot of your catch is proof enough and is a worthy trophy as memory fades and merges with dreams.

The close of the river coarse season (there is no close season for still waters any more), is always a time to reflect on the past year's fishing and to look forward to the new season. If the angler is only a coarse river fisher, he will occupy himself by repairing and renovating his tackle for the next season. Rods will be varnished and re-whipped, reels overhauled and broken tackle mended or replaced. It is also the time for looking for new waters, to extend the repertoire for that constant search for larger fish. A time to join new angling clubs, make maps and plans for the following season. The fishing season will seem to take a lifetime to come around again. Others may take this opportunity to go overseas to fish foreign waters.

Notes

Trout There is no better time than spring to fish for trout. If experienced the angler can fish all year round. A day's trout fishing, if it goes well, is perhaps the best of all angling. But I'm sad to say that, for many reasons, I don't have many good days! Some days it seems that everything is against me. Perhaps I'd forgotten my packed lunch or my fly is constantly getting hooked and caught. I like to fish uncrowded places, and usually this means overgrown rivers and small streams – not that I mind. It's an added adventure, but it also means lots of tangled line, snapped leaders and lost flies. It makes me want to tear my hair out when I've lost a fly up a tree, tie a new one on and then lose it first cast! I know then that the day isn't going to be good…

There is quite a lot of snobbery in favour of brown trout. The rainbow trout is condemned as an intruder in bastions of English fly fishing such as the Test, Kennet and Ichen.

Notes

Notes

Since the last war, the rainbow trout has become the bane of British angling.

Chris Yates, *The Secret Carp*

I can see their point of view, but now any farmer or landowner with some spare cash is quick to make a stocked rainbow trout lake. (I'm afraid carp are going the same way). The spirit of both trout and carp fishing is being lost to these landowners who thirst for profit and who grow fish by force-feeding on high-nutrient pellets. For most anglers it is a dream to catch a really big fish of double figures, but surely the worth of this fish is lost if it's 'man-made'. To catch a wild trout of just a couple of pounds gives me a greater sense of achievement.

Notes

Notes

For purists and traditionalists there will always be somewhere off the beaten track, a stretch of river which nobody knows about, or a pond forgotten by the landowner to whom it belongs. To find these places all you have to do is look and then write very nice letters to the owners. Usually arrangements can be made!

New lakes have all the modern facilities such as toilets, shops, picnic areas. These provide the family day out appeal. Non-fishers can walk, sit, picnic and sunbathe. If anglers want progress then this will become the norm. But I've read recently about an indoor fishing complex, which will make fishing more popular with the media – I can see it on the television now. As an angler, the choice is always there. You can choose between commercial angling or, like me, get away from it all on quiet streams, rivers and ponds.

Quite often when I fish remote rivers and ponds I will see no one at all. This is one thing I love about angling. It gives you time to think and to be alone. The ideal getaway. I find, if I fish alone, I can concentrate more and so increase my catch. Also, other anglers make too much noise for my liking. As with everyone, if a friend fishes with me, I find I spend far too much time talking and so lose my concentration. Having said that, though, the magical moments when you catch a huge fish are always worth sharing with a friend.

Notes

Sometimes, if the rules allow, I will fish using a worm. With a coarse fishing rod and centre-pin reel or a fly rod and flyline but with a hook on the leader instead of a fly. Worming for trout can quite often bring many different varieties of fish, which can be a wonderful surprise or a great disappointment!

I was once fishing for carp in a very old estate lake and had spent hours waiting for the carp. When I did get a bite it turned out to be a rainbow which had escaped from a trout farm up the valley. I spoke to the trout farmer about it and he said that, when the trout had spawned, some fry had escaped over the overflow and had followed the river down its course to the lake I was fishing. I believe this is how some rainbow trout have got into the rivers.

Notes

Notes

Have you ever 'tickled' a trout? This is a poaching tradition probably as old as the human race. It's a hunting instinct which fits in quite naturally with the environment. I have tried it and it's very exhilarating. You have the uncertainty of feeling a fish, which can arrive like an electric shock or it can be frightening as you never know if it might be a pike! But you must also always keep one eye over your shoulder for the bailiff or police. Today, many prime salmon rivers are 'wired' to the police and have 24-hour guards who use infrared at night to spot poachers. (Of course, this is half the fun – plotting and planning to trick the keepers and their dogs!)

I got married this summer. My local pub, aptly called 'The Rod and Line' was doing the bar for us and the landlord, knowing what a keen fisher I am, 'arranged' for us two tickled 'harvest peel' (sea trout) for our wedding breakfast. We paired them with vintage champagne and both were deliciously memorable!

Notes

Notes

Spinning for trout is another deadly method. What makes them so attracted to the spinner? Could it be that they think it's a smaller fish? A friend of mine, says its the cannibalistic nature of trout. It seems as if the fish go after it without thinking. The colour and sparkle brings out their aggressive character. It could be argued that this is also the case for pike when they chase anything with the colour red, which I was always told was supposed to represent the fins of rudd or roach. I'm not so sure now.

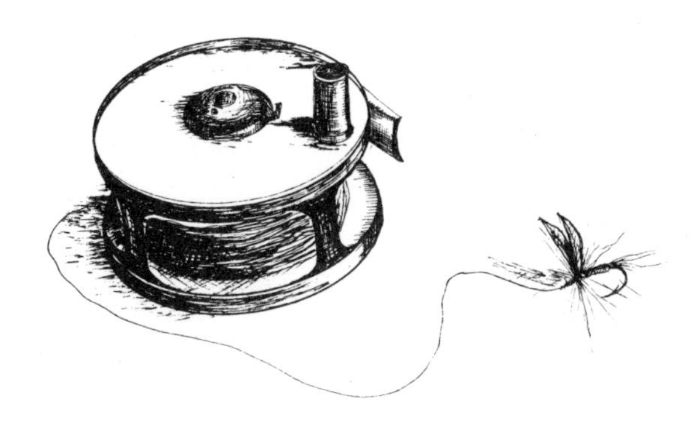

I have spent many wonderful spring days slowly spinning with small fly spoons, catching small brown trout in a local river. I sometimes ask myself why I limit my catch by fly fishing when worms and spinners are so successful. I can catch double the amount of fish worming and spinning and, after all is said and done, I do go fishing to catch fish! The answer lies in the ethics of fishing. The moral side, if you like. To catch a big trout on fly, particularly a fly you've tied yourself and to your own design, is a far more satisfying achievement than catching the same fish with a worm or spinner.

Notes

When you catch a fish on fly you are the master - completely in control. You have selected the right fly for the 'hatch', time of year, water and weather conditions. You've expertly presented the fly to the rising trout with precision and skill. Anyone can catch a big trout with a worm or spinner, but only a good and experienced angler or a very lucky one can catch a big trout with a fly.

I don't worm, spin or troll because catching fish by these methods give me far less satisfaction.

Benjamin Perkins, *At the Water's Edge*

I can't write about fly fishing for trout without mentioning the flies themselves. Fly tying is just another aspect of this great sport. To tie flies on a dark winter's night, when spring seems so far away, is very cosy, and, as my wall clock gently ticks, it seems a timeless occupation. Fly tying is a hobby which, even if angling were banned, I'd still do. Like collecting old fishing tackle, although I've always argued that I'm a fisher, not a collector.

Notes

There is a scientist in every game fisher. Entomology, the study of insects, provides us with the knowledge of what time of year certain insects turn from the nymph stage of their life cycle to the adult winged stage. As fly tiers, we try to copy them to fool the trout. The names of tied flies are so evocative – Parmachene Bell, Invicta, Bibio, Wickham's Fancy. There are lure flies like Muddler Minnow, Marabou, Matuka, Dog Nobbler, The Ace of Spades and dry flies, such as the Royal Wulf, Elk Hair Hopper, Yellow Humpy, Black Bivisable, Quill Gordon and my favourite name, a nymph, The Swannundaze. What a wonderful name!

Everyone who ties flies experiments with their own ideas. From wool pulled from the front room carpet to family pets wandering around with bald patches. I had a very fluffy ginger cat (Bob) when I was younger. His hair made a very successful nymph which I called 'Bob's Tail'. The materials we fly-tiers use is also very interesting, like partridge, peacock, goose, chicken, duck and many other birds' feathers. I've used feathers from kingfisher and heron. The amateur tier finds many rare or interesting materials when fishing – feathers from birds of prey, owls, buzzards, fur of rabbits and other small wild animals. The list is endless.

Summer

Tench Early summer is my favourite time for tench fishing. I've fished for tench for such a long time. I usually pre-bait a swim with maggots and sweetcorn and I drag the bottom with a rake head to stir up the bottom and increase the natural food supply. I do all this the night before I want to fish. Then, at dawn, I return.

The dawnscape always makes me want to get up early every day, but somehow a warm bed usually wins. The dew is heavy on the ground and can make your feet wet very quickly. From out of the semi-darkness, birds erupt into the dawn chorus and there in front of you lies the pond, a farm pool which looks dark green in the subdued light. The sun highlights freshly grown leaves with a warm glint of light and makes the water steam, giving the pool an almost eerie atmosphere. If all has gone well, your stretch of water should be covered in small bubbles, tiny dots on the flat water surface indicating that the tench are feeding.

Summer Mornings

The cold dawn
awakes my skin.
A misty start,
around a waterlily fringed pond.
A perfect mid-summer's morning.

Bubbles.
Hundreds and thousands,
but small,
like pin heads.

A scarlet tipped float
alights the waterscape.
Dipping and lifting,
indicating a hidden world.
One where no man has seen.

A fish,
a green iridescent,
high-glossed friend.
The tench,
so wondrous is its eye
it seems to glow,
a warm red,
redder than any berry.
A friend I've spent most of my life with.
A medical cure for all things on earth.

Notes

Fishing can now begin. Sometimes I will ledger or I'll float fish. Quite often I use both methods at once. This will depend on how big the tench are and how easy they are to catch. If I'm catching them ten a penny, then one rod is sufficient, another rod would be a handful, but if I were fishing for specimen tench, which are harder to catch, I would use two rods ledgering. This is my least favourite way to fish. A float lights the gloom - it dips to signal a fish.

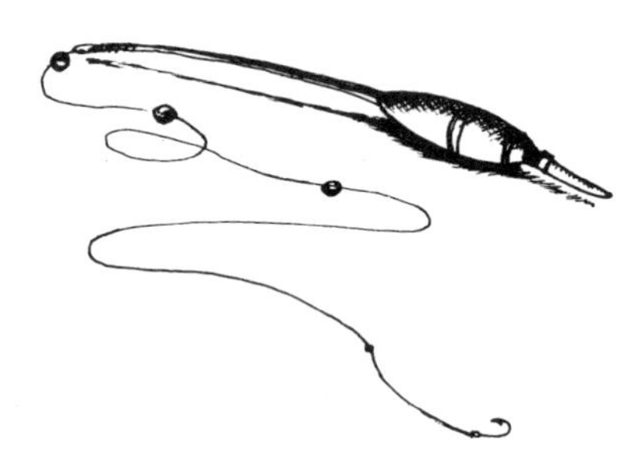

The float is pleasing in appearance and even more pleasing in disappearance.

H T Sheringham

Notes

As tench are bottom feeders, a very good method of catching them is with the lift method. This way the bait is on the bottom, and a short way from the bait, also on the bottom, is a split shot which cocks the float. When the tench takes the bait it lifts up the shot, causing the float to rise and signalling a bite. This is when you strike. A moment too soon or too late and the tench will be off.

Notes

To sit with the newly rising sun brings me great joy. The world is fresh, new and alive. At times like this I always think of B B's famous writing:

The wonder of the World, the beauty and the power,
the shapes of things, their colours, lights and shades.
These I saw, look ye also while life lasts.

B B, *Confessions of a Carp Fisher*

Notes

There seems to me to be never enough time to do all the fishing I want. With so much to do and to see, this quotation from B B always reminds me to enjoy every second I spend out in the countryside.

I have found the tench to be a very powerful fish. I would go so far as to say that, pound for pound, the tench is more powerful than the carp. Tench have very powerful pectoral fins which sometimes they seem to use as brakes to foil the angler trying to reel them in.

Notes

Apart from using the lift method, ledgering is often the best method for catching tench. Light ledger rods are best and good, reliable fixed-spool reels. A lot of people use electronic bite alarms to alert them to a bite. Long-distance ledgering fished throughout the night can usually sort out the bigger fish. Sweetcorn is the most popular bait, but now, with the carp fishing, bait explosion, many anglers are turning to boilies, about which I'll go into more detail later. Another fine method is using a frame feeder or swim feeder, which allows a ground bait or a bed of maggots to be very close to the hook bait.

The tench was always known as the doctor fish, because it was supposed to heal wounded and ill fish. It was understood for many years that pike would never attack tench, though this has been proved wrong many times over. There have been sightings of a shoal of perch rubbing themselves against a tench. It seemed to onlookers as if the perch were being healed by the powers of the tench.

In every tench's head there are two little stones which foreign physicians make great use of.

Izaak Walton, *The Compleat Angler*

Notes

I have also read stories of how tench have cured humans. One story is of a man in Rome seeing a 'great cure' done by applying a tench to the feet of a very sick man. Although it is very hard to prove that they have healing properties, as an angler I feel immediately protected from the stresses of life when I go tench fishing.

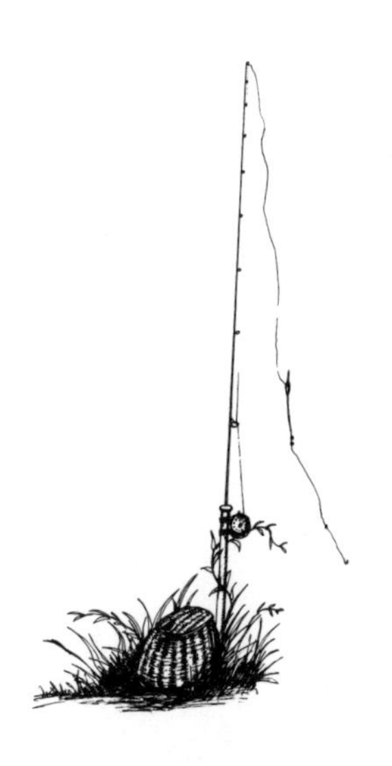

Tench not only inhabit waterlily-filled still waters, they can also be found in rivers and canals. Even in fast-flowing rivers the tench seems to be happy. It is without question one of the hardiest of all fish. It has been known for tench to live in mud when there has been serious drought. They also survive serious pollution and deoxygenation.

To me, tench fishing has everything to offer, with much shorter intervals between fish than with carp fishing. Weeks and months can go by without catching a carp. Tench, on the other hand, can be caught quite easily and one morning's fishing can produce many fine fish.

Bream Sometimes bream can be caught while tench fishing as most fish will eat the same sort of bait. Fishing at my local pond one evening I had raked a swim and was using float-fished bread flake. The warm summer evening was charged with anticipation, with a heavy, humid drizzle which is usually ideal fishing weather. The tench, I could see, had been busy feeding, and the water was dark and cloudy with the churned-up mud. I had already caught two small tench when my float dipped under. I struck and felt that living wall of power as a big fish swam away with all its might. After a while I had won the fight and reeled, to my delight, my biggest ever bream - over six pounds!

Notes

Notes

Bream also love sweetcorn, maggots, worms and luncheon meat. The tackle used is very much like that for tench fishing. Swim feeding, using a swingtip rod, is a well-proven method. A swingtip is a twelve-inch extension piece to the rod which screws into the tip's eye. It hangs loosely down by a strip of rubber. The fishing line is then passed through the rod as normal and through the eyes on the swingtip. When the swim feeder and bait are tied on and cast out, the angler watches the swingtip, which is pointing down freely towards the ground. When a fish bites and disturbs the bait, the swingtip moves, indicating a bite. The angler then strikes to connect with the fish.

In the summer sun I have seen bream sunbathe close to the water's surface, their dorsal fins breaking the water. But I have never known one to take a bait from the surface. I seem to remember someone telling me how to catch bream with a dry fly. In one pond I fish, two large bream, bigger than I have ever caught, are always on the surface during the hot summer months. I've tried many different ways of catching them but still they evade me.

Quite often in my fishing life I become obsessed by certain fish I've seen. Something seems to click and all my other angling stops while I try to realise the obsession. These two bream are one such obsession. I've given up great days carp fishing to try to catch them but, as yet…nothing! Angling is very much like this. It's about fulfilling dreams. One day I'll catch those bream and, when I do, do you think the obsession will leave me? No, I'll just become addicted to trying to capture another uncatchable dream. Like the huge rudd I've seen in a small overgrown pool, or that legendary cannibal pike which lurks in every fisherman's mind – or a record-size fish.

Notes

Notes

I think that every fisherman dreams about catching a record fish. Imagine the scene if you broke the salmon record, or pike record, or carp record. Think of the fame and fortune. The front page news with the photograph of you holding the special fish. I've often wondered what it would be like. I can see the good points, but I'm sure I'd also get a great feeling of loss. It may be something of a letdown. I'd feel that some part of my dream had gone, perhaps taking the magic with it. Would you then want to catch a bigger one to break your own record? Would you forget everything else in your life in search of that big one? Or would you lose the enthusiasm and fish for something different? In many ways I hope I never get the chance to find out!

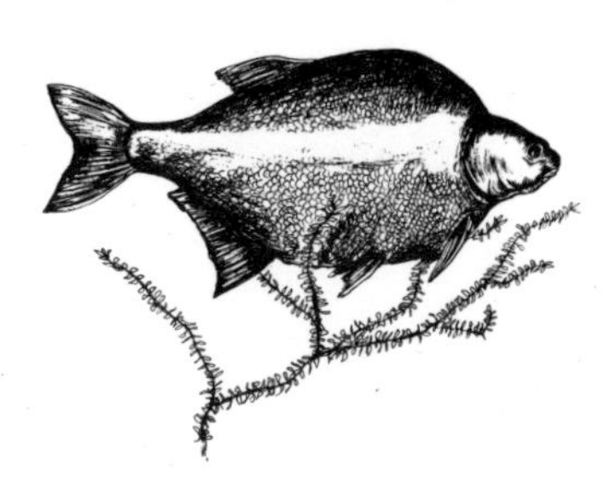

One of the finest places you'll catch a large number of good-sized bream and tench is Ireland. With a name like O'Reilly you'd expect me to say that. I have a lot of relations around Athlone - my grandfather's brother, Ambrose, owns several of the pubs there. Athlone is close to the River Shannon, which has a huge reputation for its bream and pike. Many of the lakes of Ireland hold tench, bream, huge rudd and pike, but hardly anywhere can you find carp. It's the Irish angler's dream to fish for carp. Many lakes are unfished and untapped. They are remote and uninhabited by people, a paradise for the rambling angler. (But possibly hell for the wife of the rambling angler!)

Notes

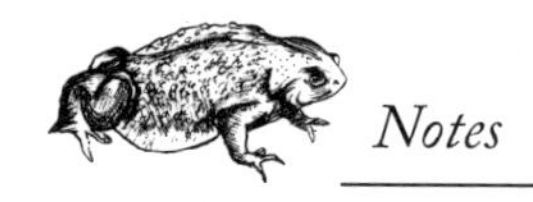

Notes

How nice it would be to go on a grand tour of famous fishing waters. Many anglers choose to go abroad in search of massive fish but I think that anglers don't explore the waters in their own country enough. There are, in angling literature, thousands of well-known English fisheries that you read about time after time. The Royalty, Redmire, the Norfolk Broads, Savay, the Test, Tring, Throop, Rutland, the Tay, the Tweed, Avington, the Lake District, the Wye and many, many others. Wouldn't it be good to have the money to spend a year on the road, staying in fine country hotels and fishing at such noble and grand places with the ghosts of the famous fishers of the past?

The brightness of summer, its warmth, lifts the spirits. Everything always looks so much better in the sun. My garden is in full bloom. I live in a cottage surrounded by a Victorian walled garden and three large orchards. I seem to be spending more time gardening nowadays than I do fishing. This only makes me appreciate what time I do have at the waterside. Having a lifetime's experience of fishing, I know, going by the weather, if I'll catch a fish or not. This means that, if I'm doubtful of catching a fish, I can stay at home and work on the garden, but if the weather is right then everything, including my paid work, is put to one side and I'll go fishing.

Notes

Rudd As summer creeps on, one of my favourite fish comes on form – the rudd. The bigger the better! They are such pretty fish, particularly if their silver scales have a glint of gold. Their fins, redder than any berry, are a vivid colour which, combined with that golden tint, is one of the finest forms of freshwater beauty. On the top of their body, by the dorsal fin, the colouring can be almost olive-green and, as any artist knows, red is the most complementary colour for green.

Notes

Notes

The biggest rudd I caught was by accident. As with my biggest bream, I was fishing tench with bread flake, close to a fallen tree, a haunt which all fish like. My quill float slid away under the water. I pulled up hard on my rod, and the fish, as expected, rushed towards the trees. I had to use a lot of side strain to compensate and pull the fish around. Soon I had won the fight and I pushed out my landing net to bring the fish in. I was amazed at the size of it. I lifted it out and I could feel the plumpness. Its scales were as large as my fingernails and it weighed 3lb 4oz - a big rudd.

The rudd is in the family of fish known as Cyprinids. This family includes carp, barbel, tench, bream and roach. A lot of inexperienced anglers find it hard to tell the difference between roach and rudd. A poet once said:

> '...A kind of roach all tinged with Gold
> Strong, broad and thick, most lovely to behold.'

Notes

One easy way to spot the difference is the fact that the rudd's dorsal fin is further down the back than on the roach. The roach also has a red colour in the iris of its eye and the rudd has yellow. There are a number of more scientific ways to tell the difference, for determining whether a fish is a rudd/roach hybrid, including a scale count and tooth count. Another way to differentiate between a rudd and a roach is to look at the lips. The rudd's lower lip sticks out further than the upper, the roach is the opposite.

Notes

Notes

Usually, if I fish for rudd I like a long float rod. Most of my rudd fishing is in still waters so I use a fixed-spool reel. I catapult out a ground bait of mashed bread, which attracts the fish in, and sometimes I'll add maggots to the mixture and a touch of milk. I use a float with all the split shot around its bottom then, using a small hook (18 or 16), I pinch onto a small flake of bread and cast towards the ground baited area. With no weight on the bottom of the hooklink the bait gently and naturally falls through the water like the ground bait.

Another method which attracts fish well is tethering a woman's hairnet full of bread close to reeds or weed. The rudd swim underneath it and on the surface, feeding off the bits which fall off. Then, using the same float set-up as before, cast as close as you can to the floating net and the rudd will be easily caught. The big rudd always seem to stay away from the main shoal, either in deeper water, feeding on scraps the others have missed, or close to the reeds. If you cast wider than normal once in a while, sometimes the bigger ones can be caught.

Notes

On hot summer days, it can be fun fly fishing for rudd, as they are quite often sunbathing. If there's room to cast, or a boat available, then a nine-foot rod and a floating line, with either a bare hook with maggots on it or a fly such as The Coachman, Blackgnat, Soldier Palmer or Little Duster, are all equally good.

Notes

I sometimes fish for rudd using my twelve-foot Indian canoe. Because of its turned-up ends, it catches the wind, which can sometimes be a problem, but on gentle summer days I lie face down and use a bamboo pole with a line and hook attached and I can silently drift with the breeze right over the shoals of rudd.

Then I just freeline a maggot or a piece of bread flake down amongst them and catch one every cast. If I were to use my oar the splashing would cause far too much disruption of the water and scare the rudd away. This method, I've found, is also very good for stalking carp in weed. On hot days carp find themselves pockets of weed to bask in. It's very hard to reach them from the bank, but drifting near by canoe and then freelining a worm to them using a carp rod and centre-pin is much more successful. With a centre-pin there is no bale arm to click over and, when you're trying to be quiet, the loud sound of metal clicking is the last thing you want.

Notes

Eel A fish that always bites well in the summer is the eel. I'm not talking of small ones, which really irritate match anglers. I mean the really big specimens! I find the eel very interesting mainly because not many people fish for them. I always like to be different, but I'm sure if people knew how a five-pound eel could fight there would be a lot more eel fishers.

Notes 

Notes

Trees which fall into the water provide the eel with a home, and this is certainly the best place to catch them. Big lob worms or half-sections of small rudd or roach are the best baits. I use my carp ledger tackle to catch them. The only difference is that I use a ten-pound wire trace as big eels have big teeth!

I fish two rods at a time, a bobbin placed between the reel and the butt eye. If I'm fishing at night I will use an electronic buzzer I made myself, which is a copy of Richard Walker's prototype Heron bite alarm. I hardly ever use a ground bait. I should do more often but I feel that it only attracts small eels. If I do use ground bait I will use a bigger hook bait. You will know when eels are in your swim and interested in your bait by the way the bobbin will twitch and lift a little. This will happen a lot. I feel sure that it is small eels after the bait. But quite often, after this nerve-wracking time of not knowing whether to strike or not, the line will rush out, causing the bobbin to rise with such speed it will hit the underneath of the rod. Then is the time to strike! Often, I'm left reeling in the line as it is small eels who can't eat the bait, so when I strike it pulls the bait away from them. If I'm lucky it might be a big one.

Notes

Notes

Any eel over two and a half pounds is a good catch. When a large eel is landed you can feel the strength in its body as you wrestle to unhook it. The biggest I have caught, nearly six pounds, was as thick as my wrist. It was a typical eel evening – humid, sticky. It was drizzling and the air was thick with the promise of thunder. I caught two three-pound fish before the eel twice that size.

One fishing trip I was using the last section of very small roach, which I had injected with pilchard oil to give a strong scent. I was just thinking about going home when the bobbin shot upwards. I struck, and felt my rod bend with such force that I thought I'd got a carp. I fought as if I'd hooked the devil, and seeing my catch, a giant eel as it surfaced gave me quite a fright. I was almost scared to land it. Even with my carp landing net, it was hard to get it in.

Notes

I am sure that the pond from which I caught this eel contains eels over ten pounds. An estuary runs a few hundred yards away and big eels must come up the dyke which leads to the pond. Eels can also travel great distances overland.

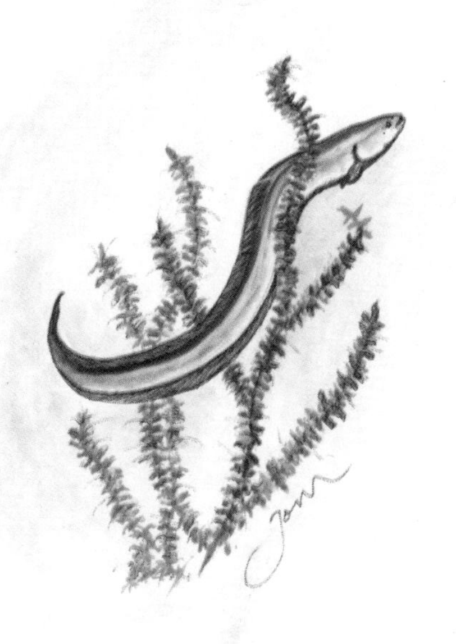

Notes

Not fashionable amongst the fishing fraternity, eels are often very badly treated. Countless times I've rescued them, after anglers have abandoned them, in disgust. I've seen anglers cut the eel's stomach open when it has still been alive, just to retrieve the hook.

Eels travel thousands of miles in their lifetime. In their first three years they leave the spawning area in the Sargasso Sea, near the Gulf of Mexico, to arrive as elvers on our coastline. Then, during the spring, the elvers swim in large numbers up the estuaries to the freshwater ponds and rivers. After all this, some mindless angler kills an eel just because it tangles his precious line. It makes me so angry! Of all our freshwater fish, I think the eel deserves the most respect. When the eel reaches fresh water it stays there for seven to nine years and then makes its way back to the Sargasso Sea to spawn. It always migrates during the night, usually when there's a storm and no moon and in the months of September and October.

Notes

Eels were the first fish I caught when I was a boy. I would lift up stones in a small stream near to where I lived. Under the rocks were elvers but occasionally I would find a big eel, weighing about a pound. It terrified me, making me jump and run. This is why I find eel fishing so fascinating. I'm overcoming my childhood terror by catching large ones!

Notes

Autumn

Carp The leaves slowly change colour to the bronzes and yellows of autumn. In our beautiful country there is no better time to fish. Many species seem to be at their most active before the slow semi-hibernation of winter. I spend a lot of time fishing for carp in the summer using baits which float on the surface but, as the sun loses its heat, the carp sink into the dark deeps.

Notes

The carp is an ancient fish. It came to England in the Middle Ages from Europe and Asia.

Hops and turkeys, carp and beer
Came into England all in a year!

The Chronicle of Sir Richard Baker, 1530

Notes

Notes

Carp mostly live in still waters and sometimes in slow rivers. A quiet, overgrown estate pond is often the haunt of big carp. Many were introduced into such stately ponds to help keep the pond weed down, which grass carp, in particular, do very well. These types of ponds gave birth to the sport of carp fishing. The pioneers of carp fishing all started by fishing in these wonderful old ponds.

One particular pool stands out among all others – Redmire Pool in Herefordshire. Redmire was stocked in 1934 by Donald Leney, a fish farmer in Surrey who imported a Galician strain of carp (from the Galicia region of Poland). These fish, of mixed mirror and common variety, can grow to a massive size. In Britain the record at present stands at over fifty pounds. This is a huge fish by any standards but on the Continent, and in Africa, Asia, the US and Canada, carp can grow to over eighty pounds!

Notes

In 1951, Bob Richards caught a record carp from Redmire weighing 31lb 4oz. This led to a friendship between him and the great anglers and writers B B, Richard Walker and Peter Thomas. A year later, on 13 September, Walker caught the most famous coarse fish of all time; Clarissa, a forty-four pound common carp, also from Redmire. This captured the angling world's imagination and soon carp fishing was to blossom, with more and more anglers involved. Redmire, this small two and three quarter acre pool, became England's premier carp water. Every year huge fish are sighted and rumours of a king of all carp, abound. Then, in 1980, on the first day of the opening season, Chris Yates caught a mirror carp of 51lb 6oz, which knocked Clarissa from the top of the record books.

Carp Pond

The pond lies immense.
Weed islands float yellow and green.
Trees overhang…some fallen others just old.
A boyhood passion rekindled.

On the bank. Fern and hazel.
Bamboo, tall, straight and high.
High enough for a fisher boy to make a den.

Lily pads, seem solid, firm and supportive.
A black shadow comes close to the surfacc.
A carp.
The sun highlighting mud colour fins.
Golden flanks.
Its mighty dorsal fin penetrates the water
echoing ripples.
The passions ablaze.
Through boy's eyes I saw my first carp.

At this same pond.
Months and years have passed.
The carp are bigger, older and wiser.
We've all aged.
The passion remains the same.

Now the monsters at Redmire have all slowly disappeared. The biggest seen today is about thirty-five pounds. Will Redmire ever produce a record fish again? Is the king still alive? It's hard to say. The younger fish are growing fast. In ten years' time there might be another sixty-pounder swimming about. Carp fishing today has moved on from small ponds to huge gravel pits and lakes. Fish stocked in these grow quickly and very large. These are the future of big carp angling.

Notes

Notes

A man who fishes habitually for carp has a strange look in his eyes...[as] if he had been to heaven or hell.

Arthur Ransome

I started carp fishing at a very early age. I was privileged enough to live less than a hundred yards away from one of the finest carp ponds in Cornwall. This is where I served my apprenticeship to coarse fishing. The carp have grown with me, old friends now, whom I know and love. The Pond, as I call it, is still as it was when I was a child. I fish there most weeks and the angling club which leases the Pond has made me an honorary bailiff. The carp here are of average size - the biggest I've named Dando.

Notes

Notes

I try to fish very simply, preferring a stalking approach over the static. Today, many anglers wait patiently behind three or four rods, ledgering at long distance, waiting for the fish to come to them.

The 'stalking' approach allows the angler to go to the fish, to find them and move with them. On an autumn day, you might find them feeding in the shallows, churning and sifting through the bottom for blood worms or cruising underneath the overhang of bushes and bankside vegetation. The static ledgering approach would try to cast to these places from further down the bank or even from another side of the pool. The stalker, on the other hand, actually creeps and crawls amongst the undergrowth to get within a few feet of his quarry. Utter silence is called for and concealment, so as not to scare the fish. I've heard of dedicated anglers putting mud on their faces to camouflage themselves and even to tie branches on their clothes so as to blend in more effectively with the background.

Notes

Once the fish has been found, the bait can be cast - usually a simple bait, sometimes a natural one like worms so the carp think that it has just fallen into the water from one of the branches overhead. A carp in these conditions loses a bit of its caution as it's not used to being caught out in this manner. A good, strong rod is needed. I use a ten-foot rod made by Agutters of Ashford, Kent, England. My reel is usually a fixed-spool with a ten-pound line. In this case a fixed-spool reel is far superior to a centre-pin because of the drag, which can be tightened right up to stop the carp heading for any obstructions nearby.

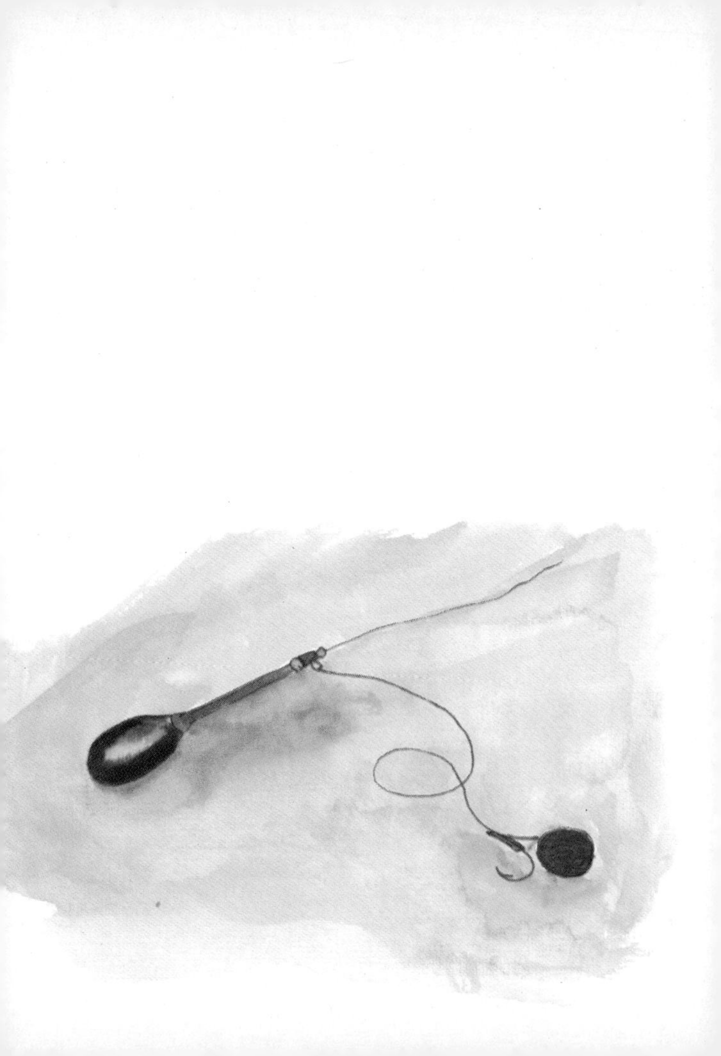

It's amazing to see carp feed at close range while you are stalking, watching their reaction to certain baits and reading their body language. I've seen carp pick up bait with the hook inside it and then spit it out very fast - it's most infuriating!

This is why the 'hair rig' was invented. The bait is attached via a one-inch hair to the eye of the hook and moves freely when a carp picks it up. As the fish spits the bait out, the hook catches on the carp's lip and so the carp hooks itself. But I have seen, at Redmire, a very clever fish pick up a hair-rigged bait and not get hooked! Carp are such intelligent fish. They seem to be able to learn from their mistakes and I'm sure by others'. Over the years, carp have come to recognise baits that have been used a lot before. Baits, therefore, are constantly evolving. Old baits like bread and sweetcorn are being replaced by exotic beans and pulses. Tiger nuts and boilies are some of the best baits.

Notes

Boilies have grown from the late sixties' simple baits which were made from wheatgerm to today's mixture, some of which dissolve in water. Boilies are made up of proteins, fats, carbohydrates, minerals, vitamins and flavourings, which give the carp a highly nutritious food. In theory, the carp are meant to eat these because they consist of everything they need to live on, which saves them finding a lot of natural food. The carp might be very clever but it can also be very lazy.

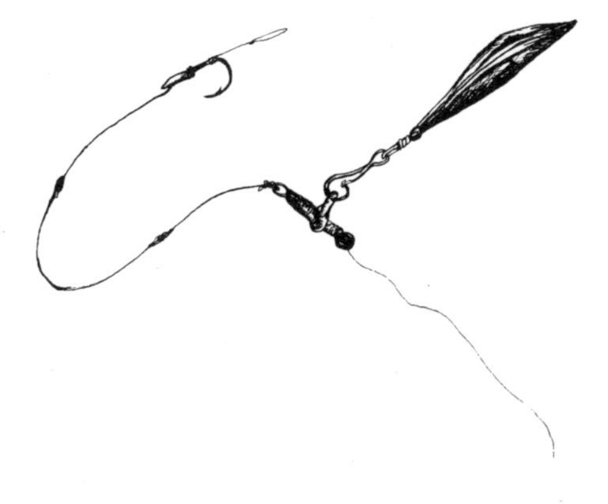

If a bait is put in front of a fish, it's more likely to take it than not. If it's there, it's less trouble to eat the fisherman's bait than to look for its own food. In some places carp are very wise and wary of boilies, so much so that they are more willing to take baits like bread than boilies. So old baits can't be dismissed completely. Anyway, I'm sure, as Hugh Sheringham wrote, 'So far as my experience goes, it is certain that good luck is the most vital part of the equipment of him who would seek to slay big carp.'

Notes

A carp in autumn is in the peak of condition and looks splendid. A large common carp will look like a bronzed knight in shining armour and will fight with passion and as gallantly as St George. The mirror carp can show colours of orange and ochre, reflecting the colours of an autumn day or the sunset which follows. Out of the two I have no favourite. I'm as pleased with one as with the other and to me the size is less important than you may think. Any size fish is better than none at all! But, as with all anglers I have my targets, my dreams and my hopes. Some I've already attained, others I may never attain. This feeling of anticipation is why I fish. Every time I go fishing I can never be sure what, if anything, I'll catch.

Sometimes, perhaps if you're very lucky, once a year you might realise some goal, such as catching a three-pound perch which you have seen many times before, or catching the biggest known carp in your local lake. After you've reached your goal you set yourself new and more exciting ones.

The carp angler is always in search of bigger carp, from vague rumours of a pool with a thirty-pounder, to private clubs and syndicates who don't publicise the fact that they have huge fish so as not to attract the 'wrong kind' of angler. How many anglers are contented with their local rivers and pools? At one time, before the car made new waters easy to find and get to, the angler only fished rivers and still waters within walking or cycling distance of his home. Nowadays there is an enormous choice of fishing venues but is our fishing really any better? I'm sure in your local waters there are specimens, big fish which have never been caught. Who's to say that the biggest fish caught in your local pools are not the biggest ever caught?

Notes

On hot days, carp can clearly be seen basking on the surface, particularly near Canadian weed or waterlilies. When the carp are in this mood I employ one of my favourite methods of catching them. That is, with the floating bait method, either using floating bread crust or pre-soaked 'Chum mixer'. Mixers float very well and can be flavoured. My preferred flavouring is maple or oriental spice. A float is attached three feet away from the hook and bait. The line in between is creased to make a float. The floats are usually heavy and self-cocking, and if the water is very clear I use bubble floats. I cast as near to the carp as I can without scaring them away, then catapult out a few free offerings. Now comes the excitement. Watching the carp as they come to take the bait is breathtaking and heart stopping.

Notes

Seeing those rubberlike lips open up to take your bait is one of the biggest highs in fishing. When the mighty fish swallows and dips it is time to strike! Nine out of ten times I will be left reeling in my float and missing bait, but sometimes I connect with that unseen living power. My reel screams with pain as that first rush drags the line out with such speed and ferocity that I feel I'm about to be pulled into the water.

On many occasions I have felt that nothing I can do will stop the carp on its first run. I'm left shaking, sweating and angry if my line snaps. Losing a fish is a horrible moment in every angler's life and is something we can't resolve. You can try using a heavier rod or line and losing the clutch on your reel, but something, if your luck is low, will always happen. I've had my line caught in trees, bale arms snapping and breaking on reels, fish losing themselves in weed, line grating on stones, fish falling off at the landing net, hooks becoming untied, drag sticking on my reel and, the worst way of all of losing a fish, the hook simply coming out! You can't blame anything or anyone and that experience of loss is unimaginable to the non-angler. It's hard to explain how bad you feel - completely numb, paralysed, dumbfounded. It sometimes makes you hate fishing for a period when you remember all the other things that went wrong on that day. But I've always believed that it's better to have played and lost than never to have played at all.

Salmon Another very autumnal fish is the salmon. The salmon river is a beautiful place at this time of year. There is a great deal of snobbery associated with catching salmon. It seems you are higher in the angling hierarchy if you fish for them with a fly than if you use worms. Again, this is wrong. There is just as much skill in careful touch ledgering as there is in a roll cast or spey cast. Touch ledgering is such a subtle way of fishing, and can also be used to great effect when fishing for barbel and chub.

Notes

Notes

With salmon, you use a prawn or worm, weighted down by a drilled bullet about twelve inches from the hook. When this is cast you hold the line with your thumb and index finger and you can then feel the vibrations on the line when the fish bites. It's a very natural, delicate and simple way of fishing. I'm sure the fingers are far more sensitive than any electronic bite alarm. Every movement of the bait can be felt. It's great to visualise the bait slowly drifting about, over rocks and stones, through weed, and then to feel the fish take - it sends electricity up the line and into your hands. Float fishing can also be very successful in catching salmon, though I think that touch ledgering will indicate a hooked fish quicker than the float because it's direct.

Salmon Weir

Spray
and
foam.
A leap,
a return.
A deafening,
vibrant,
power.

Silver,
determination.
Another
struggle:
and return.
Bubbles,
mist,
a cold steam.
A cold stream.

Highland
daze,
excitement
and
wonder.

Rocks,
the rawness.
A
jump,
a
fall.

All
to spawn.

The river in autumn: the golden colour of the beech trees and chestnuts, the yellow and fawn of the reeds and bulrushes and that endless sound of the water which is sometimes quiet for just a minute to match the surrounding silence.

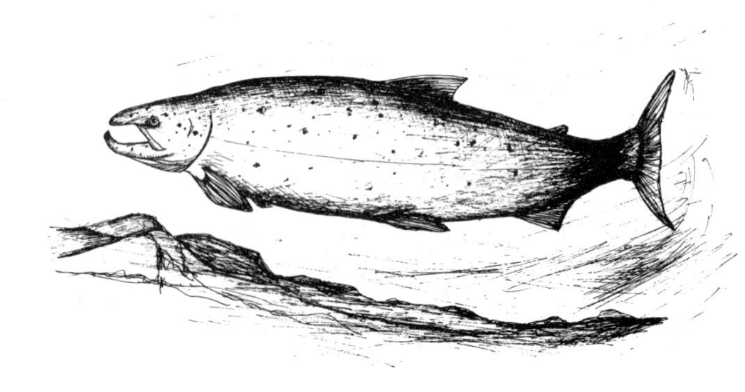

Notes

To walk on a cool autumn evening after a day at the river, with crows cawing and the sound of a distant fox, fills me with such emotion. It is times like this which make me glad to be alive. Being outside in such beauty is, for me, what angling is all about.

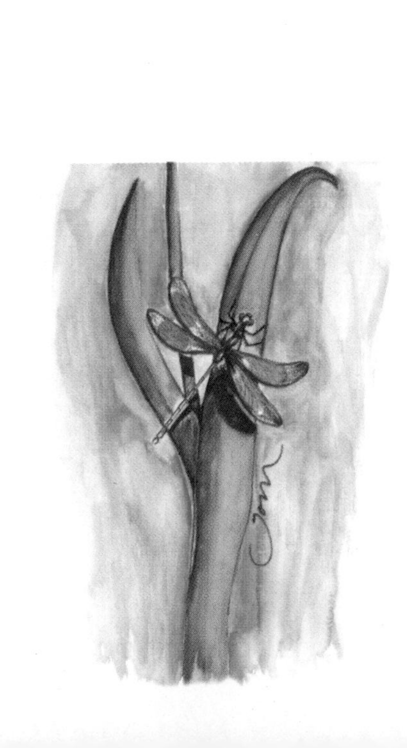

Notes

A wonderful story was published in the *Badminton Library Book* about salmon. It tells of a Major Maurice Hallahan, who, while fishing in a very deep pool in the Blackwater of County Cork, hooked a very large salmon. The salmon towed him and his boat a great distance. When at last the fish was tired, the Major gaffed the fish, which struggled so much that he let go of it, at which point the line snapped and the fish swam away. A year later the Major fished the same pool, caught the same salmon and found his lost gaff still in the fish's side. The shaft of the gaff had sprouted!

Will the salmon record made by Miss G W Ballantyne on 7 October 1922 ever be broken? The fish weighed a massive sixty-four pounds! I can only assume that this achievement won't be surpassed. Rivers today are getting more and more polluted and filled with toxic acid rain. There are also the commercial net fishermen, who have very sophisticated methods. I can remember one story of a poacher who tickled a salmon which weighed far more than the record, but as he shouldn't have been in possession of the fish, he couldn't claim the credit.

Notes

Winter

Pike & Perch The still waters and rivers in autumn and winter are good times to catch perch. The long shadows of the evenings will draw me to the reeds and rushes, which are the favourite haunt of perch. They are very pretty fish and remind me of the first fish I caught as a child.

My biggest perch, caught while writing this book, was caught on bread flake, which is a very strange bait for catching perch. I was after rudd at dusk. I think the perch was attracted by the colour and movement. This perch weighed over two and a half pounds, my most notable fish of the year so far and the equivalent of a twenty-five pound carp or salmon! Worms are the perch's favourite bait, along with maggots, fry and sometimes spinners. I've heard of perch even taking smaller perch.

Notes

Notes

The same can be said of pike, who have been known to choke to death by eating other pike as big as themselves. This strange and hardly believable act is known as Union Jack. Dr Crull mentions that in 1698 a pike was taken with an infant child in its stomach! A pike will eat just about anything which is in its domain, from fish to water rats to ducklings, even, or so I've read, a small dog. People bathing in its path have had their arms bitten and their fingers snapped at. It is the freshwater tiger shark. This is its mystery and why it is liked so much by anglers. It fights with so much aggression so, with this in mind, dead fish baits, live fish baits and spinners, lures and plugs are the best ways to trigger the pike's aggression.

Pike can be found in many rivers, canals and most still waters, apart from here in Cornwall, which, I'm sad to say, doesn't offer much pike fishing at all. I travel fifty miles or more into Devon to fish pike. I use my carp fishing tackle which I've found to be ideal. I prefer boat fishing to bank fishing. It just seems somehow right and also allows me to explore the water, trying out different places.

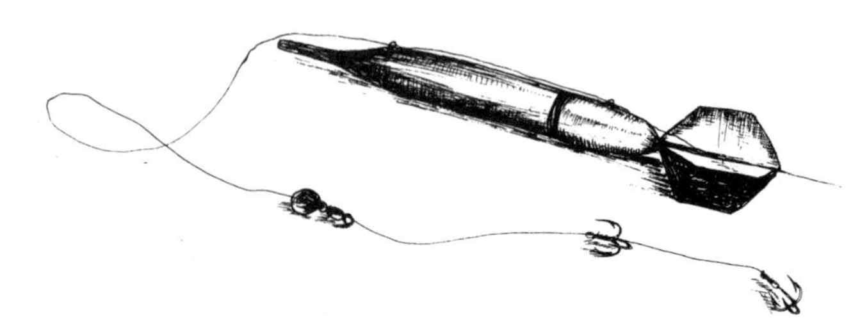

Notes

Notes

One of my favourite methods of catching pike is to 'wobble' a dead fish as if it were still alive. The fish, usually a small rudd or roach, is mounted on snap tackle and then cast out and slowly retrieved, stopping reeling every now and again to make the dead bait waver and appear to the pike to be alive.

The next step up from this is spinning with large spoons, spinners, plugs and even flies. Like floats and flies, plugs are a type of fishing equipment which I always like to collect and to hold. Their strange shapes and bright colours are a joy to look at. The ones I like best are Big Hedds and Prowlers. Spinners are also fascinating to watch moving over the water.

Notes

A Camouflaged Beauty

Sunlight pierces the water,
sending shafts of light.
Highlighting contours,
reed, weed and silt.

There.
Remaining very still,
void of life,
lies the pike.
Waiting.
A camouflaged beauty.
A historic villain
in wait.
Its gills open and close.
It's alive.
Waiting.
Alert but still.
Waiting.
A glint of silver drifts by.
Swimming,
without a care.
Waiting.
Gone!

Notes

As winter bites hard and snow and frost cover the earth in sparkling white, other fish completely lose their appetite and go into a lethargic state of semi-hibernation. Tench are known to bury themselves in the muddy bottom.

Notes

Notes

I was once on my Indian canoe and found a tench which was covered with leeches. As I picked it up from where it had been resting in the shallows, it seemed to be half asleep. It made no attempt to get away - it was very docile and floppy, like a newborn baby after its feed. When I let it go, it righted itself and then dipped down to the bed again.

Pike and winter go together as tench and summer. On dry, cold, winter days, when you can see your breath on the air, pike fishing is at its best. And there is no better way to enjoy the winter landscape. Pike fishing from a boat is very active, not only from rowing but also from spinning. How many times I cast in a day I don't know. It keeps the cold from biting too hard, though!

Notes

Notes

Pike are found throughout the world. The US and Canada offer brilliant sport. In Germany, with their salmon all gone, pike is their number one game fish. The River Rhine holds massive fish. Ireland is also a pike fisher's paradise, where 'the fish have bites as hard as the drink'. The Norfolk Broads have massive examples and somewhere hiding away is the grand master. Loch Lomond in Scotland shelters enormous pike. Here famous angler and writer Fred Buller once lost one, witnessed by four experienced anglers, weighing over fifty pounds. And what about all the big trout reservoirs where coarse anglers aren't allowed to fish? I'm sure, there must be record-size fish of all types.

In Ireland, in the *Limerick Chronicle* of May 1862, there was reported a pike which was caught on rod and line, weighing ninety and a half pounds. There have also been records of two pike, both weighing over seventy pounds, caught in the 1800s. In England we did hear rumours of a sixty-pounder, or at least over fifty pounds. How many bigger ones have been found dead? As I've said, the biggest fish caught in a water aren't necessarily the biggest there. It's this continual hope that drives fishermen after that bigger one. Every day I hear rumours and stories of big fish...most I take with a pinch of salt, but in a small number of cases there is an element of truth. How many times have you been told by a local fisher boy, his hair unkempt, his nose running or red, his clothes dirty, covered in eel slime and ground bait, that just the other day he saw a fish as big as him or his dog?

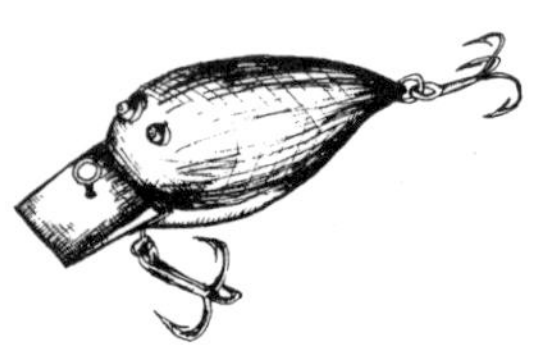

Notes

Notes

With pike and carp fishing there is always mystery. What lurks in those dark depths? Nobody can really be sure. If you're faced with an Irish lough or large reservoir it's easy to believe that somewhere in there is that fish of a lifetime. All your angling targets achieved with one almighty fish. In such huge expanses of water the uncertainty is so great that it's easy to tremble with fright at the thought. I know of an old copper mine in Devon, 200 feet deep and surrounded by beech trees. It is a terrifying and daunting place, quite disturbing as you peer down the sheer sides and wonder what's at the bottom.

Notes

Not everyone likes pike. I find them fascinating, a very regal and proud fish. But salmon and trout anglers hate then as they spoil their fisheries. They are persecuted and hunted as killers of small salmon and trout, which in no way solves the problem.

In the River Dee they had a problem with pike and slaughtered all the big ones. This, however, only made matters worse, as these big pike who ate the small salmon would also kill 'jack' pike. The result was an explosion in the pike population as the small pike had no enemies to eat them. In many ways there is a great divide between coarse and game anglers. I wrote the following poem to illustrate this:

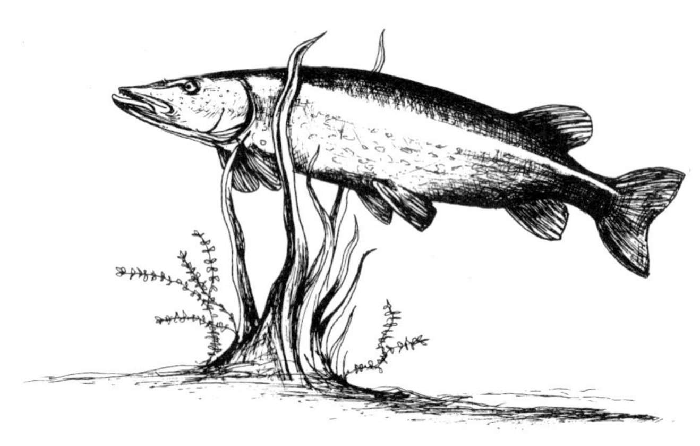

Notes

The Prince of the River

Autumn.
The golden time of the year,
crisp days with long shadows,
give the river a timeless quality.
As cold fingers try to cast.
A world filled with brown,
yellow and gold.
A time for wonder,
enjoyment of the environment;
and for barbel.

The noble prince of the river.
A romantic fish,
of elegant line,
stream lined,
A dashing hero,
strong and true.

Chub are its men-at-arms,
who pledge allegiance to the prince,
inseparable
and valiant.
Ready to fight.
To knock the king from his throne.

The mighty salmon surrounded by his dignitaries,
and page boys.
The prime minister,
the sea trout;
and armies of rainbows and browns.

In my eyes the prince
is the true king.
The salmon,
an invader.
Who pillaged and robbed
his way to supremacy.

Perhaps the prince needs help?
From the pike?
A fearless bounty hunter,
not to be trusted.
A fish
to get the job done.
A fish
that takes no sides.
Who is lord of the river.
A moody warrior,
who takes no prisoners.

Eels and perch,
are his servants.
Both are vicious and blood hungry.
Willing to die for the pike,
not for the prince.
But for the right price
they can be bought.

This struggle will go on forever,
as long as there is game and coarse.

Notes

Chub Apart from pike, the other notable good winter fish are chub and grayling. Here in Cornwall it is always a few degrees warmer than the rest of England. Many of our coarse fish stay more active than those further north. In fact, looking into my catch records, I see that I catch more and bigger carp in the autumn and winter months than I do in spring and summer. I put this down to angling pressure. In the summer months the fish have more anglers trying to catch them, so they are shy and very cautious of unnatural baits. In the winter they are less fished for (some anglers stay at home, thinking they won't catch anything), so the carp drop their guard a little.

Tom

Notes

I find the chub to be a very fickle fish. Some days, fishing in the same spot with the same bait, I will catch a netful – other days, nothing at all. But isn't this the same with all fishing? On the coldest of cold days, when the earth takes on a white blanket, the chub is quite often the only fish that will bite. They will take any bait you put to them, from worms and maggots, sweetcorn and cheese, small fish and slugs to bacon rind and cherries. I even heard of using rabbits' stomachs and bullocks' brains! Lures, spinners and flies will catch one. As with baits, most methods will be successful, from ledgering to fly fishing, floater fishing to floating bait fishing.

The chub is found in most rivers and a few in still waters. One famous chub was called Popeye and was caught in that holy of holies, Redmire Pool. It weighed close to five and a half pounds and proves that chub do well in still water.

A good chub is about four pounds, which is the equivalent of a twenty-five pound salmon. I always use this method of describing the sizes of fish to anglers. As a twenty-five pound carp looks big, some anglers think a three-pound rudd is a small fish in comparison. But if you know the national records for each fish, the rudd is the equivalent of a thirty-pound carp! On the Continent, chub have grown to near twenty pounds.

Notes

Notes

Reflections

One of the best things about winter fishing is coming home after a cold day. I step through the front door and am greeted with a warm fire, an even warmer smile and a hot cup of tea. I have fished since I was a child and I hope I always will.

Angling becomes a way of life and, if I could, I'd fish every day, rain or shine. I am, I admit, addicted to angling. Whenever I'm doing something else I will certainly be thinking about fishing my favourite ponds or rivers, about my tackle or about the fish themselves and how I shall next try to catch them.

Notes

The spirit of angling has entered my body and soul. The cuts and scratches I've suffered have absorbed fish slime. My mouth has taken in the rivers and ponds I fish. I've been drunk on the water of life created by these fabulous places, these epicentres of nature, and become 'high' on the smell of a landed fish. That fix of adrenaline keeps me sane and in a good frame of mind. To fish on winter days clears the cobwebs in my mind. Angling is a wonderful drug!

There are so many reasons why I fish, of which only a small number have been included in this small volume. To overcome the barriers of pleasure and pain, to confront all the preconceived ideas about angling, to be non-conformist and anarchistic is the way forward. To do the unexpected will bring the angler his biggest prize! Angling means so many different things to many different people, from the long vigil of the long-stay carp angler to the action packed stillwater fly angler. It's the countless variations that make angling such a wonderful sport.

Notes

Notes

It's my world and I don't want any other. What it hasn't got isn't worth having and what it doesn't know it isn't worth knowing.

Ratty talking to Mole about The River, Kenneth Grahame, *The Wind in the Willows*

Notes

Notes

Published by MQ Publications Ltd
254-258 Goswell Road, London EC1V 7EB

ISBN: 1-897954-10-7

Printed and bound in Hong Kong